Beginning DevOps with Docker

Automate the deployment of your environment with the power of the Docker toolchain

Joseph Muli

BIRMINGHAM - MUMBAI

Beginning DevOps with Docker

Acquisition Editor: Koushik Sen
Content Development Editor: Darren Patel
Production Coordinators: Vishal Pawar, Samita Warang

First published: May 2018

Production reference: 1310518

Published by Packt Publishing Ltd.

Livery Place

35 Livery Street

Birmingham B3 2PB, UK.

ISBN 978-1-78953-240-1

www.packtpub.com

`mapt.io`

Mapt is an online digital library that gives you full access to over 5,000 books and videos, as well as industry leading tools to help you plan your personal development and advance your career. For more information, please visit our website.

Why subscribe?

- Spend less time learning and more time coding with practical eBooks and Videos from over 4,000 industry professionals

- Learn better with Skill Plans built especially for you

- Get a free eBook or video every month

- Mapt is fully searchable

- Copy and paste, print, and bookmark content

PacktPub.com

Did you know that Packt offers eBook versions of every book published, with PDF and ePub files available? You can upgrade to the eBook version at `www.PacktPub.com` and as a print book customer, you are entitled to a discount on the eBook copy. Get in touch with us at `service@packtpub.com` for more details.

At `www.PacktPub.com`, you can also read a collection of free technical articles, sign up for a range of free newsletters, and receive exclusive discounts and offers on Packt books and eBooks.

Contributors

About the author

Joseph Muli is a DevOps engineer with three years of experience of extensive innovation and development. He has worked with Python and Bash, building a deep love for scripting and automation. He's currently focusing on monitoring, logging, and maintenance, three key data reference points in any environment.

You can get in touch with him on GitHub: mrmuli or on Twitter: @the_codeartist.

About the reviewer

John Kariuki has been developing software that helps migrate to a scalable microservice architecture for over 11 years now. He founded a start-up straight out of campus and has been a prominent member of the tech community in Nairobi. Outside of programming, John has an interest in writing blog posts and photography.

He's currently placed with First Access, an Andela partner and New York based credit scoring and profiling platform for microlenders in emerging markets.

Packt is searching for authors like you

If you're interested in becoming an author for Packt, please visit authors.packtpub.com and apply today. We have worked with thousands of developers and tech professionals, just like you, to help them share their insight with the global tech community. You can make a general application, apply for a specific hot topic that we are recruiting an author for, or submit your own idea.

Table of Contents

Preface

DevOps with Docker outlines the power of containerization and the influence this innovation has on development teams and general operations. We also get to understand what DevOps really is, the principles involved, and how the process contributes to product health, by implementing a Docker workflow. Docker is an open source containerization tool that makes it easier to streamline product delivery and reduce the time it takes to get from a whiteboard sketch of the business to a money-back implementation.

The book will provide knowledge of the following:

- Docker and DevOps and why and how they integrate
- What containers are, and how to create and manage them
- Scaling a delivery pipeline and multiple deployments with Docker
- Orchestration and delivery of containerized applications

What This Book Covers

Lesson 1, Images and Containers, shows how Docker improved a DevOps workflow and the basic Docker terminal commands that will be used in this book. We will learn the Dockerfile syntax in order to build images. We will run containers from images. We will then version images and Docker hub and deploy a Docker image to the Docker hub.

Lesson 2, Application Container Management, explores the docker-compose tool and gives an overview of a multi-container application setup. We will then manage multiple containers and distribute application bundles. Lastly, we will network with docker-compose.

Lesson 3, Orchestration and Delivery, gives us an overview of a Docker Swarm. We will then use the Docker engine to create a Swarm and manage services and applications in a Swarm. Finally, we will scale services up and down to test for a real-world application scenario.

What You Need for This Book

Hardware

This book will require the following minimum hardware requirements:

- Processor: 1.8 GHz or higher (Core 2 Duo and above)
- Memory: Minimum 2GB RAM
- Hard disk: Minimum 10 GB
- A stable internet connection (for pulling and pushing images)

Software

- Operating System: Windows 8 or higher
- Browser: Google Chrome or Mozilla Firefox (latest updates installed)
- Docker installed

Who This Book is for

This book is ideal for developers, system architects, junior and mid-level site reliability engineers who wish to adopt Docker workflow for consistency, speed, and isolation in applications. You need to have a basic knowledge about UNIX concepts such as ssh, ports, and logs as we dive into Docker.

Conventions

In this book, you will find a number of text styles that distinguish between different kinds of information. Here are some examples of these styles and an explanation of their meaning.

Code words in text, database table names, folder names, filenames, file extensions, pathnames, dummy URLs, user input, and Twitter handles are shown as follows: "Once you have created a new directory, access the directory and create a file called run.js."

Any command-line input or output is written as follows:

```
docker pull
```

New terms and **important words** are shown in bold. Words that you see on the screen, for example, in menus or dialog boxes, appear in the text like this: "Clicking the Next button moves you to the next screen."

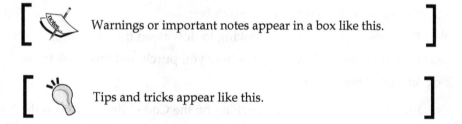

Warnings or important notes appear in a box like this.

Tips and tricks appear like this.

Reader Feedback

Feedback from our readers is always welcome. Let us know what you think about this book—what you liked or disliked. Reader feedback is important for us as it helps us develop titles that you will really get the most out of.

To send us general feedback, simply e-mail `feedback@packtpub.com`, and mention the book's title in the subject of your message.

If there is a topic that you have expertise in and you are interested in either writing or contributing to a book, see our author guide at `www.packtpub.com/authors`.

Customer Support

Now that you are the proud owner of a Packt book, we have a number of things to help you to get the most from your purchase.

Downloading the Example Code

You can download the example code files for this book from your account at `https://github.com/TrainingByPackt/Beginning-DevOps-with-Docker`. If you purchased this book elsewhere, you can visit `http://www.packtpub.com/support` and register to have the files e-mailed directly to you.

You can download the code files by following these steps:

1. Log in or register to our website using your e-mail address and password.
2. Hover the mouse pointer on the **SUPPORT** tab at the top.
3. Click on **Code Downloads** & **Errata**.
4. Enter the name of the book in the **Search** box.
5. Select the book for which you're looking to download the code files.
6. Choose from the drop-down menu where you purchased this book from.
7. Click on **Code Download**.

You can also download the code files by clicking on the **Code Files** button on the book's webpage at the Packt Publishing website. This page can be accessed by entering the book's name in the **Search** box. Please note that you need to be logged in to your Packt account.

Once the file is downloaded, please make sure that you unzip or extract the folder using the latest version of:

- WinRAR / 7-Zip for Windows
- Zipeg / iZip / UnRarX for Mac

- 7-Zip / PeaZip for Linux

The code bundle for the book is also hosted on GitHub at `https://github.com/PacktPublishing/`. We also have other code bundles from our rich catalog of books and videos available at `https://github.com/PacktPublishing/`. Check them out!

Installation

Before you start with this course, we'll install Docker. You will find the steps to install it here:

Visit to the Docker Toolbox page below: `https://docs.docker.com/toolbox/toolbox_install_windows/` in your browser.

1. Click the installer link to download.
2. Install Docker Toolbox by double-clicking the installer.
3. Press Next to accept all the defaults and then install.

Errata

Although we have taken every care to ensure the accuracy of our content, mistakes do happen. If you find a mistake in one of our books — maybe a mistake in the text or the code — we would be grateful if you could report this to us. By doing so, you can save other readers from frustration and help us improve subsequent versions of this book. If you find any errata, please report them by visiting `http://www.packtpub.com/submit-errata`, selecting your book, clicking on the Errata Submission Form link, and entering the details of your errata. Once your errata are verified, your submission will be accepted and the errata will be uploaded to our website or added to any list of existing errata under the **Errata** section of that title.

To view the previously submitted errata, go to `https://www.packtpub.com/books/content/support` and enter the name of the book in the search field. The required information will appear under the **Errata** section.

Piracy

Piracy of copyrighted material on the Internet is an ongoing problem across all media. At Packt, we take the protection of our copyright and licenses very seriously. If you come across any illegal copies of our works in any form on the Internet, please provide us with the location address or website name immediately so that we can pursue a remedy.

Please contact us at `copyright@packtpub.com` with a link to the suspected pirated material.

We appreciate your help in protecting our authors and our ability to bring you valuable content.

Questions

If you have a problem with any aspect of this book, you can contact us at `questions@packtpub.com`, and we will do our best to address the problem.

1

Images and Containers

This lesson will cover fundamental concepts about containerization as a foundation for the images and containers we will later build. We will also get to understand how and why Docker gets involved in the DevOps ecosystem. Before we begin, we will see how virtualization differs from containerization in Docker.

Lesson Objectives

By the end of this lesson, you will be able to:

- Describe how Docker improves a DevOps workflow
- Interpret Dockerfile syntax
- Build images
- Set up containers and images
- Set up a local dynamic environment
- Run applications in Docker containers
- Obtain a basic overview of how Docker manages images via Docker Hub
- Deploy a Docker image to Docker Hub

Virtualization versus Containerization

This block diagram gives an overview of a typical virtual machine setup:

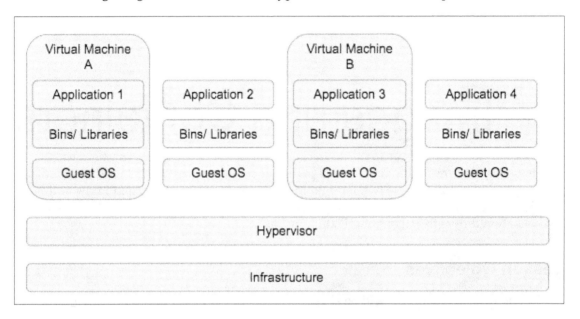

In virtual machines, the physical hardware is abstracted, therefore we have many servers running on one server. A hypervisor helps do this.

Virtual machines do sometimes take time to start up and are expensive in capacity (they can be GBs in size), although the greatest advantage they have over containers is the ability to run different Linux distributions such as CentOS instead of just Ubuntu:

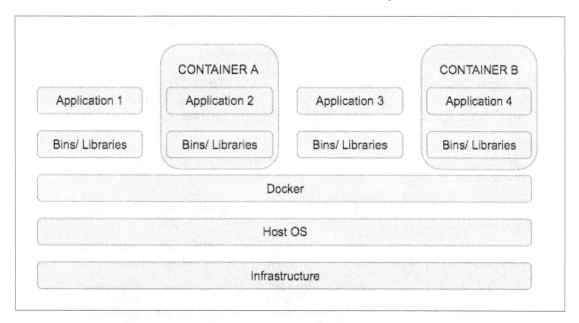

In containerization, it is only the app layer (where code and dependencies are packaged) that is abstracted, making it possible for many containers to run on the same OS kernel but on separate user space.

Containers use less space and boot fast. This makes development easier, since you can delete and start up containers on the fly without considering how much server or developer working space you have.

Let's begin the lesson with a quick overview on how Docker comes into play in a DevOps workflow and the Docker environment.

How Docker Improves a DevOps Workflow

DevOps is a mindset, a culture, and a way of thinking. The ultimate goal is to always improve and automate processes as much as possible. In layman language, DevOps requires one to think in the laziest point of view, which puts most, if not all, processes as automatic as possible.

Docker is an open source containerization platform that improves the shipping process of a development life cycle. Note it is neither a replacement for the already existing platforms nor does the organization want it to be.

Docker abstracts the complexity of configuration management like Puppet. With this kind of setup, shell scripts become unnecessary. Docker can also be used on small or large deployments, from a hello world application to a full-fledged production server.

As a developer on different levels, whether beginner or expert, you may have used Docker and you didn't even realize it. If you have set up a continuous integration pipeline to run your tests online, most servers use Docker to build and run your tests.

Docker has gained a lot of support in the tech community because of its agility and, as such, a lot of organizations are running containers for their services. Such organizations include the following:

- Continuous integration and continuous delivery platforms such as Circle CI, Travis CI, and Codeship
- Cloud platforms such as **Amazon Web Services (AWS)** and **Google Cloud Platform (GCP)** allow developers to run applications out of containers
- Cisco and the Alibaba group also run some of their services in containers

Docker's place in the DevOps workflow involves, but is not limited to, the following:

Examples of Docker's use cases in a development workflow.

Unifying requirements refers to using a single configuration file. Docker abstracts and limits requirements to a single Dockerfile file.

Abstraction of OS means one doesn't need to worry about building the OS because there exist prebuilt images.

Velocity has to define a Dockerfile and build containers to test in, or use an already built image without writing a Dockerfile.Docker allows development teams to avoid investment on steep learning curves through shell scripts because "automation tool X" is too complicated.

Recap of the Docker Environment

We walked through the fundamentals of containerization earlier. Allow me to emphasize the alternative workflow that Docker brings to us.

Normally, we have two pieces to a working application: the project code base and the provisioning script. The code base is the application code. It is managed by version control and hosted in GitHub, among other platforms.

The provisioning script could be a simple shell script to be run in a host machine, which could be anywhere from a Windows workstation to a fully dedicated server in the cloud.

Using Docker does not interfere with the project code base, but innovates on the provisioning aspect, improving the workflow and delivery velocity. This is a sample setup of how Docker implements this:

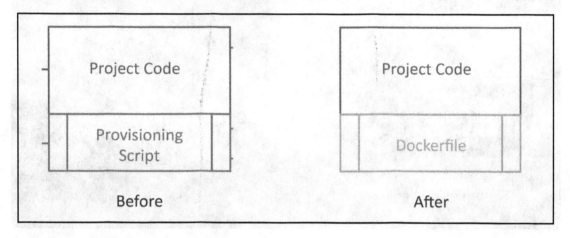

The **Dockerfile** takes the place of the provisioning script. The two combined (project code and Dockerfile) make a **Docker image.** A Docker image can be run as an application. This running application sourced from a Docker image is called a **Docker container.**

The Docker container allows us to run the application in a completely new environment on our computers, which is completely disposable. What does this mean?

It means that we are able to declare and run Linux or any other operating system on our computers and then, run our application in it. This also emphasizes that we can build and run the container as many times as we want without interfering with our computer's configuration.

With this, I have brought to your attention four key words: **image, container, build**, and **run**. We will get to the nitty-gritty of the Docker CLI next.

Basic Docker Terminal Commands

Open Command Prompt to check that Docker is installed in your workstation. Entering the command `docker` on your terminal should show the following:

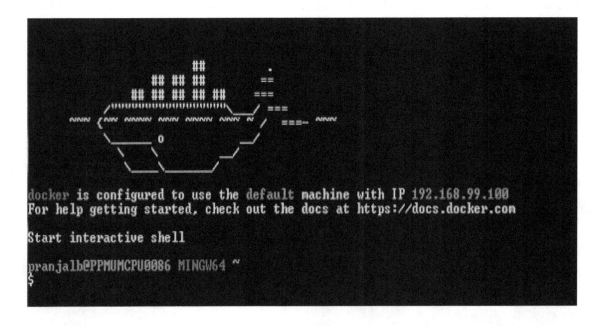

This is the list of available subcommands for Docker. To understand what each subcommand does, enter `docker-subcommand -help` on the terminal:

→ **devops-for-docker** docker

Usage: docker COMMAND

A self-sufficient runtime for containers

Options:

Run `docker info` and note the following:

- Containers
- Images
- Server Version

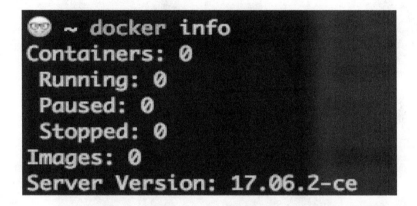

This command displays system-wide information. The server version number is important at times, especially when new releases introduce something that is not backward-compatible. Docker has stable and edge releases for their Community Edition.

We will now look at a few commonly used commands.

This command searches **Docker Hub** for images:

```
docker search <term> (for example, docker search ubuntu)
```

Docker Hub is the default Docker registry. A Docker registry holds named Docker images. Docker Hub is basically the "GitHub for Docker images". Earlier, we looked at running an Ubuntu container without building one; this is where the Ubuntu image is stored and versioned:

"There are private Docker registries, and it is important that you are aware of this now."? Docker Hub is at `hub.docker.com`. Some images are hosted at `store.docker.com` but Docker Store contains official images. However, it mainly focuses on the commercial aspect of an app store of sorts for Docker images and provides workflows for use.

The register page is as shown here:

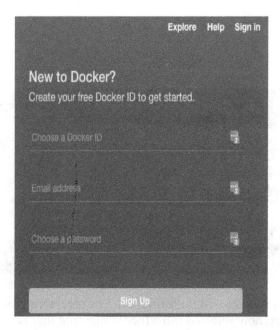

The log in page is as shown here:

From the results, you can tell how users have rated the image by the number of stars. You can also tell whether the image is official. This means that the image is promoted by the registry, in this case, Docker Hub. New Docker users are advised to use official images since they have great documentation, are secure, promote best practices, and are designed for most use cases. As soon as you have settled on one image, you'll need to have it locally.

 Ensure you are able to search for at least one image from Docker Hub. Image variety ranges from operating systems to libraries, such as Ubuntu, Node.js, and Apache.

This command allows you to search from Docker Hub:

```
docker search <term>
```

For example, `docker search ubuntu`.

This command pulls an image from the registry to your local machine:

```
docker pull
```

For example, `docker pull ubuntu`.

As soon as this command is running, you'll notice that it is using the default tag: `latest`. In Docker Hub, you can see the list of tags. For **Ubuntu**, they are listed here: `https://hub.docker.com/r/library/ubuntu/` plus their respective Dockerfiles:

```
 ~ docker pull ubuntu
Using default tag: latest
latest: Pulling from library/ubuntu
ae79f2514705: Downloading [=>                                      ]  982.3kB/47.62MB
c59d01a7e4ca: Download complete
41ba73a9054d: Verifying Checksum
f1bbfd495cc1: Download complete
0c346f7223e2: Download complete
```

Download the Ubuntu image profile on Docker Hub from:
`https://hub.docker.com/r/library/ubuntu/`.

Activity 1 — Utilizing the docker pull Command

To get you conversant with the `docker pull` command.

The goal of this activity is to gain a firm understanding of the `docker-pull` CLI, not only by running the listed commands, but also by seeking help on other commands while exploring, through manipulating the built containers.

1. Is Docker up and running? Type `docker` on the terminal or command-line application.
2. This command is used to pull the image from the Docker Hub.

    `docker pull`

Image variety ranges from operating systems to libraries, such as Ubuntu, Node.js, and Apache. This command allows you to pull images from Docker Hub:

For example, `docker pull ubuntu`.

This command lists the Docker images we have locally:

*   `docker images`

When we run the command, if we have pulled images from Docker Hub, we will be able to see a list of images:

They are listed according to the repository, tag, image ID, date created, and size. The repository is simply the image name unless it is sourced from a different registry. In this case, you'll have a URL without the `http://` and the **top level domain (TLD)** such as `registry.heroku.com/<image-name>` from the Heroku registry.

This command will check whether the image by the name `hello-world` exists locally:

    docker run <image>

For example, `docker run hello-world`:

```
 ~ docker run hello-world
Unable to find image 'hello-world:latest' locally
latest: Pulling from library/hello-world
9a0669468bf7: Pull complete
Digest: sha256:cf2f6d004a59f7c18ec89df311cf0f6a1c714ec924eebcbfdd759a669b90e711
Status: Downloaded newer image for hello-world:latest

Hello from Docker!
This message shows that your installation appears to be working correctly.
```

If the image is not local, it will be pulled from the default registry, Docker Hub, and run as a container, by default.

This command lists the running containers:

    docker ps

If there aren't any running containers, you should have a blank screen with the headers:

```
 ~ docker ps
CONTAINER ID    IMAGE        COMMAND        CREATED        STATUS        PORTS        NAMES
 ~ 
```

Activity 2 — Analyzing the Docker CLI

Ensure you have the Docker CLI running by typing `docker` on your terminal.

You have been asked to demonstrate the commands covered so far.

To get you conversant with the Docker CLI. The goal of this activity is to gain a firm understanding of the `docker-compose` CLI, not only by running the listed commands, but also by seeking help on other commands while exploring, through manipulating the built containers. The goal is to be flexible enough with the CLI to be able to use it in a real-world scenario such as running an automated script.

1. Is Docker up and running? Type `docker` on the terminal or command-line application.

2. Search for the official Apache image using the CLI, using `docker search apache`:

3. Attempt to pull the image using `docker pull apache`.

4. Confirm the availability of the image locally using `docker images`.

5. Bonus: Run the image as a container using `docker run apache`.

6. Bonus: Stop the container using `docker stop <container ID>`.

7. Bonus: Delete the container and the image using `docker rm <container ID>`.

Dockerfile Syntax

Every Docker image starts from a **Dockerfile**. To create an image of an application or script, simply create a file called Dockerfile.

It does not have an extension and begins with a capital letter D.

A Dockerfile is a simple text document where all the commands that template a container are written. The Dockerfile always starts with a base image. It contains steps to create the application or to run the script in mind.

Before we build, let's take a quick look at a few best practices on writing Dockerfiles.

Some best practices include, but are not limited to, the following:

- **Separation of concern**: Ensure each Dockerfile is, as much as possible, focused on one goal. This will make it so much easier to reuse in multiple applications.

- **Avoid unnecessary installations**: This will reduce complexity and make the image and container compact enough.

- **Reuse already built images**: There are several built and versioned images on Docker Hub; thus, instead of implementing an already existing image, it's highly advisable to reuse by importing.

- **Have a limited number of layers**: A minimal number of layers will allow one to have a compact or smaller build. Memory is a key factor to consider when building images and containers, because this also affects the consumers of the image, or the clients.

We'll start simply with a Python and JavaScript script. The choice of these languages is based on their popularity and ease of demonstration.

Writing Dockerfiles for Python and JavaScript examples

 No prior experience is required on the selected languages as theyare meant to give a dynamic view of how any language can adopt containerization.

Python

Before we begin, create a new directory or folder; let's use this as our workspace.

Open the directory and run `docker search python`. We'll pick the official image: `python`. The official image has the value **[OK]** in the **OFFICIAL** column:

```
~ docker search python
NAME       DESCRIPTION                                  STARS   OFFICIAL   AUTOMATED
python     Python is an interpreted, interactive, obj...  2295    [OK]
django     Django is a free web application framework...   600    [OK]
```

Go to `hub.docker.com` or `store.docker.com` and search for python to get the correct tag or at least know what version the Python image with the latest tag is. We will talk more about tags in *Topic D*.

The image tag should be the number with this syntax that looks like `3.x.x` or `3.x.x-rc`.

Create a file by the name `run.py` and enter the first line as follows:

```
print("Hello Docker - PY")
```

Create a new file on the same folder level and name it **Dockerfile.**

 We do not have an extension for the Dockerfile.

Add the following in the Dockerfile:

```
FROM python
ADD . .
RUN ls
CMD python run.py
```

The **FROM** command, as alluded to earlier, specifies the base image.

The command can also be used on an inheritance point of view. This means you do not have to include extra package installations in the Dockerfile if there already exists an image with the packages.

The **ADD** command copies the specified files at source to the destination within the image's filesystem. This means the contents of the script will be copied to the directory specified.

In this case because run.py and Dockerfile are on the same level then run.py is copied to the working directory of the base image's file system that we are building upon.

The **RUN** command is executed while the image is being built. ls being run here is simply for us to see the contents of the image's filesystem.

The **CMD** command is used when a container is run based on the image we'll create using this Dockerfile. That means at the end of the Dockerfile execution, we are intending to run a container.

JavaScript

Exit the previous directory and create a new one. This one will be demonstrating a node application.

Add the following line in the script and save:

```
console.log("Hello Docker - JS")
```

Run docker search node - we'll pick the official image: node

Remember that the official image has the value **[OK]** in the **OFFICIAL** column:

```
~ docker search node
NAME                    DESCRIPTION                              STARS  OFFICIAL  AUTOMATED
node                    Node.js is a JavaScript-based platform for...  4745   [OK]
mhart/alpine-node       Minimal Node.js built on Alpine Linux    320
```

Note that node is the JavaScript runtime based on Google's high performance, open source JavaScript engine, V8.

Go to `hub.docker.com` and search for node to get the correct tag or at least know what version the node image with the latest tag is.

Create a new Dockerfile and add the following:

This should be on the same file level as the script.

```
FROM node
ADD . .
RUN ls
CMD node run.js
```

We'll cover these for now.

Activity 3 — Building the Dockerfile

Ensure you have the Docker CLI running by typing `docker` on your terminal.

To get you conversant with Dockerfile syntax. The goal of this activity is to help understand and practice working with third-party images and containers. This helps get a bigger picture on how collaboration can still be affected through containerization. This increases product delivery pace by building features or resources that already exist.

You have been asked to write a simple Dockerfile that prints `hello-world`.

1. Is Docker up and running? Type `docker` on the terminal or command-line application.
2. Create a new directory and create a new Dockerfile.

3. Write a Dockerfile that includes the following steps:

```
FROM ubuntu:xenial
RUN apt-get install -y apt-transport-https curl software-properties-
common python-software-properties
RUN curl -fsSL https://apt.dockerproject.org/gpg | apt-key add
RUN echo 'deb https://apt.dockerproject.org/repo ubuntu-xenial main'
> /etc/apt/sources.list.d/docker.list
RUN apt-get update
RUN apt-get install -y python3-pip
RUN apt-get install -y build-essential libssl-dev libffi-dev python-
dev
```

Building Images

Before we begin building images, let's understand the context first. An image is a standalone package that can run an application or allocated service. Images are built through Dockerfiles, which are templates that define how images are to be built.

A container is defined as a runtime instance or version of an image. Note this will run on your computer or the host as a completely isolated environment, which makes it disposable and viable for tasks such as testing.

With the Dockerfiles ready, let's get to the Python Dockerfile directory and build the image.

docker build

The command to build images is as follows:

```
docker build -t <image-name> <relative location of the Dockerfile>
```

-t stands for the tag. The <image-name> can include the specific tag, say, latest. It is advised that you do it this way: always tagging the image.

The relative location of the Dockerfile here would be a dot (.) to mean that the Dockerfile is on the same level as the rest of the code; that is, it is at the root level of the project. Otherwise, you would enter the directory the Dockerfile is in.

If, for example, it is in the Docker folder, you would have docker build -t <image-name> docker, or if it is in a folder higher than the root directory, you would have two dots. Two levels higher would be three dots in place of the one dot.

The output on the terminal and compare to the steps written on the Dockerfiles. You may want to have two or more Dockerfiles to configure different situations, say, a Dockerfile to build a production-ready app and another one for testing. Whatever reason you may have, Docker has the solution.

The default Dockerfile is, yes, Dockerfile. Any additional one by best practices is named `Dockerfile.<name>`, say, `Dockerfile.dev`.

To build an image using a Dockerfile aside from the default one, run the following:
`docker build -f Dockerfile.<name> -t <image-name> <relative location of the Dockerfile>`

 If you rebuild the image with a change to the Dockerfile, without specifying a different tag, a new image will be built and the previous image is named `<none>`.

The `docker` build command has several options that you can see for yourself by running `docker build --help`. Tagging images with names such as latest is also used for versioning. We will talk more on this in the *Topic F*.

To build the image, run the following command in the Python workspace:

```
>$ docker build -t python-docker .
```

 The trailing dot is an important part of the syntax here:

```
→ devops-for-docker ls
js-example        python-example
→ devops-for-docker cd python-example
→ python-example docker build -t python-docker .
```

The trailing dot is an important part of the syntax here:

```
→ devops-for-docker ls
js-example      python-example
→ devops-for-docker cd js-example
→ js-example docker build -t js-docker .
```

Open the JavaScript directory and build the JavaScript image as follows:

```
>$ docker build -t js-docker .
```

Running the commands will outline the four steps based on the four lines of commands in the Dockerfile.

Running `docker images` lists the two images you have created and any other image you had pulled before.

Removing Docker Images

The `docker rmi <image-id>` command is used to delete an image. Let me remind you that the image ID can be found by running the `docker images` command.

To delete the images that are non-tagged (assumed not to be relevant), knowledge of bash scripting comes in handy. Use the following command:

```
docker rmi $(docker images | grep "^<none>" | awk "{print $3}")
```

This simply searches for images with <none> within their row of the docker images command and returns the image IDs that are in the third column:

```
 ~ docker images
REPOSITORY          TAG             IMAGE ID            CREATED             SIZE
js-docker           latest          4e40ca9349d2        8 minutes ago       676MB
python-docker       latest          6d10adac9b37        8 minutes ago       691MB
node                latest          c1d02ac1d9b4        21 hours ago        676MB
python              latest          79e1dc9af1c1        11 days ago         691MB
ubuntu              latest          dd6f76d9cc90        12 days ago         122MB
 ~ docker rmi 4e40ca9349d2
Untagged: js-docker:latest
Deleted: sha256:4e40ca9349d251d4fa386e4bac89654a56d44581931146944b8981bb44ac23973
Deleted: sha256:8c3868e9b796d6ddeeb4b8a35712c0346a9f8a70e9da93c871e38c590c7d5786
Deleted: sha256:ad490b4ae1e3e206a9e09656c8df0dbe494726868f7958bf253d8ebaa26fcee9
Deleted: sha256:fdff661f1fc24d01980bea19a0d37b427150474d983ed9415b4f89f7c87a5175
 ~ ▌
```

Activity 4 — Utilizing the Docker Image

Ensure you have the Docker CLI running by typing docker on your terminal.

To get you conversant with running containers out of images.

You have been asked to build an image from the Dockerfile written in *Activity C*. Stop the running container, delete the image, and rebuild it using a different name.

1. Is Docker up and running? Type docker on the terminal or command-line application.
2. Open the JavaScript example directory.
3. Run docker build -t <choose a name> (observe the steps and take note of the result).
4. Run docker run <the-name-you-chose>.
5. Run docker stop <container ID>.
6. Run docker rmi <add the image ID here>.
7. Run docker build -t <choose new name>.
8. Run docker ps (note the result; the old image should not exist).

Running Containers From Images

Remember when we mentioned containers are built from images? The command `docker run <image>` creates a container based on that image. One can say that a container is a running instance of an image. Another reminder is that this image could either be local or in the registry.

Go ahead and run the already created images `docker run python-docker` and `docker run js-docker`:

```
→ python-example ls
Dockerfile run.py
→ python-example docker run python-docker
```

What do you notice? The containers run outputs to the terminal's respective lines. Notice that the command preceded by CMD in the Dockerfile is the one that runs:

```
docker build -t python-docker:test .  and docker build -t js-docker:test .
```

Then, run the following:

```
python-docker:test and docker run js-docker:test
```

 You will not see any output on the terminal.

This is not because we don't have a command CMD to run as soon as the container is up. For both images built from Python and Node, there is a CMD inherited from the base images.

 Images created always inherit from the base image.

The two containers we have run contain scripts that run once and exit. Examining the results of `docker ps`, you'll have nothing listed from the two containers run earlier. However, running `docker ps -a` reveals the containers and their state as exited.

There is a command column that shows the CMD of the image from which the container is built from.

When running a container, you can specify the name as follows:

`docker run --name <container-name> <image-name>` (for example, `docker run --name py-docker-container python-docker`):

```
→ python-example ls
Dockerfile run.py
→ python-example docker run py-docker-container py-docker
```

We outlined earlier that you only want to have relevant Docker images and not the `<none>` tagged Docker images.

As for containers, you need to be aware that you can have several containers from one image. `docker rm <container-id>` is the command for removing containers. This works for exited containers (those that are not running).

For the containers that are still running, you would have to either:

Stop the containers before removing them (`docker stop <container-id>`)

Remove the containers forcefully (`docker rm <container-id> -f`)

No container will be listed if you run `docker ps`, but sure enough if we run `docker ps -a`, you will notice that the containers are listed and their command columns will show the inherited CMD commands: `python3` and `node`:

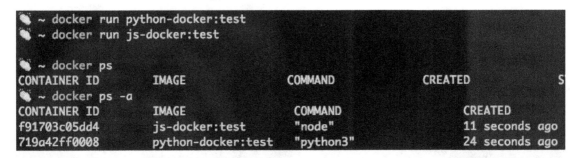

Python

The CMD in Dockerfile for Python's image is `python3`. This means that the `python3` command is run in the container and the container exits.

 With this in mind, one gets to run Python without installing Python in one's machine.

Try running this: `docker run -it python-docker:test` (with the image we created last).

We get into an interactive bash shell in the container. `-it` instructs the Docker container to create this shell. The shell runs `python3`, which is the CMD in the Python base image:

```
 ~ docker run -it python-docker:test
Python 3.6.3 (default, Nov  4 2017, 22:17:09)
[GCC 4.9.2] on linux
Type "help", "copyright", "credits" or "license" for more information.
>>>
```

In the command `docker run -it python-docker:test python3 run.py`, `python3` `run.py` is run as you would in the terminal within the container. Note that `run.py` is within the container and so runs. Running `docker run -it python python3 run.py` would indicate the absence of the `run.py` script:

```
 ~ docker run -it python-docker:test python3 run.py
Hello Docker - PY
 ~
```

```
 ~ docker run -it python python3 run.py
python3: can't open file 'run.py': [Errno 2] No such file or directory
 ~
```

The same applies to JavaScript, showing that the concept applies across the board.

`docker run -it js-docker:test` (the image we created last) will have a shell running node (the CMD in the node base image):

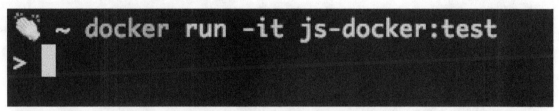

```
 ~ docker run -it js-docker:test
>
```

`docker run -it js-docker:test node run.js` will output `Hello Docker - JS`:

```
 ~ docker run -it js-docker:test node run.js
Hello Docker JS
 ~
```

That proves the inheritance factor in Docker images.

Now, return the Dockerfiles to their original state with the CMD commands on the last line.

Versioning Images and Docker Hub

Remember talking about versioning images in *Topic D*? We did that by adding latest and using some numbers against our images, such as `3.x.x` or `3.x.x-rc`.

In this topic, we'll go through using tags for versioning and look at how official images have been versioned in the past, thereby learning best practices.

The command in use here is the following:

```
docker build -t <image-name>:<tag> <relative location of the Dockerfile>
```

Say, for example, we know that Python has several versions: Python 3.6, 3.5, and so on. Node.js has several more. If you take a look at the official Node.js page on Docker Hub, you see the following at the top of the list:

9.1.0, 9.1, 9, latest (9.1/Dockerfile) (as of November 2017):

Short Description

Python is an interpreted, interactive, object-oriented, open-source programming language.

Full Description

Supported tags and respective **Dockerfile** links

Shared Tags

- `3.7.0a2`, `3.7-rc`, `rc`:
  - `3.7.0a2-stretch` *(3.7-rc/stretch/Dockerfile)*
  - `3.7.0a2-windowsservercore` *(3.7-rc/windows/windowsservercore/Dockerfile)*

This versioning system is called semver: semantic versioning. This version number has the format MAJOR, MINOR, PATCH in an incremental manner:

MAJOR: For a change that is backward-incompatible

MINOR: For when you have a backward-compatible change

PATCH: For when you make bug fixes that are backward-compatible

---

You'll notice labels such as `rc` and other prerelease and build metadata attached to the image.

When building your images, especially for release to the public or your team, using semver is the best practice.

That said, I advocate that you do this always and have this as a personal mantra: semver is key. It will remove ambiguity and confusion when working with your images.

Deploying a Docker Image to Docker Hub

Every time we run `docker build`, the image created is locally available. Normally, the Dockerfile is hosted together with the code base; therefore, on a new machine, one would need to use `docker build` to create the Docker image.

With Docker Hub, any developer has the opportunity to have a Docker image hosted to be pulled into any machine running Docker. This does two things:

- Eliminates the repetitive task of running `docker build`
- Adds an additional way of sharing your application which is simple to set up compared to sharing a link of your app's code base and **README** detailing the setup process

`docker login` is the command to run to connect to **Docker Hub** via the CLI. You need to have an account in hub.docker.com and enter the username and password through the terminal.

`docker push <docker-hub-username/image-name[:tag] >` is the command to send the image to the registry, Docker Hub:

```
→ devops-for-docker ls
js-example        python-example
→ devops-for-docker cd python-example
→ python-example ls
Dockerfile run.py
→ python-example docker push joseph.muli/new-py-example:0.1
```

A simple search of your image on `hub.docker.com` will give the output to your Docker image.

In a new machine, a simple `docker pull <docker-hub-username/your-image-name>` command will produce a copy of your image locally.

Summary

In this lesson, we have done the following:

- Reviewed the DevOps workflow and a few use cases for Docker
- Walked through Dockerfile syntax
- Gained a high-level understanding of the build images for applications and running containers
- Constructed a number of images, versioned them, and pushed them to Docker Hub

2

Application Container Management

In this lesson, we will scale one of the containers we built into a multi-tier setup. This will involve splitting the application into different logical sections. For example, we could have an application running on a Docker container and the application's data in a separate database container; however, both should work as a single entity. For this, we will use Docker's tool for running multi-container applications. The tool goes by the name `docker-compose`. In summary, `docker-compose` is the tool used for defining and running multi-container Docker applications.

Lesson Objectives

By the end of this lesson, you will be able to:

- Get an overview of a multi-container application setup
- Work through the `docker-compose` file and CLI
- Manage multiple containers and distributed application bundles
- Set up a network with `docker-compose`
- Handle and debug the different application layers

The docker-compose Tool

Let's begin the lesson by looking at what a multi-container setup is, why it is important, and how Docker, with the tool `docker-compose`, works like a charm in such scenarios.

We have recently been introduced to how applications work, with their separate elements: frontend, backend, and database.

To run such a multi-tier application using Docker, one would need to run the following commands to spin up the containers in different terminal sessions:

```
- docker run <front-end>
- docker run <back-end>
- docker run <database>
```

You can run `docker run` with (`-d`) as detached to prevent us from running the three commands in separate sessions, for example: `docker run <front-end> -d`

That said, it even becomes particularly tasking linking different containers (networking).

`docker-compose` comes in to save the day. We can define and run multi-containers from one file - `docker-compose.yml`. In the following topics, we'll discuss this further. First, let's install it.

Installing docker-compose

If you went through the installation of Docker in *Lesson 1, Images and Containers*, `docker-compose` was most likely installed with Docker. To confirm this, run `docker-compose` in your terminal.

If the command is recognized, you should have an output like the following:

```
> ~ docker-compose
Define and run multi-container applications with Docker.

Usage:
  docker-compose [-f <arg>...] [options] [COMMAND] [ARGS...]
  docker-compose -h|--help

Options:
  -f, --file FILE             Specify an alternate compose file (default: docker-compose.yml)
  -p, --project-name NAME     Specify an alternate project name (default: directory name)
  --verbose                   Show more output
  -v, --version               Print version and exit
```

Windows users should install the Community Edition of Docker to install
`docker-compose` alongside it. Docker Toolbox includes `docker-compose` in its installation.

> For further `docker-compose` installation steps, check out the
> documentation at: `https://docs.docker.com/compose/install/`.
>
> While on this subject, please note the various ways of uninstalling it. In
> order to uninstall the program:
>
> Go to **Programs and Features**.
>
> Look for Docker, right-click, and **Uninstall**.

Overview of a Multi-Container Application Setup

In the previous lesson, we introduced Docker and containerization. We ran sample Python
and JavaScript scripts as demonstrations of how applications can be containerized and how
images can be built. We are now ready to run an application that goes beyond that.

In a Dockerfile, every line describes a layer. The union filesystem used in Docker allows
different directories to transparently overlay, forming a single, coherent filesystem. The
foundational layer is always an image which you build upon. Each additional line with
a command, say, RUN, CMD, and so on, adds a layer to it. The advantage of layers is
that as long as the layer has not been modified, it will not bother building that part of the
image. Secondly, as an image is pulled from a Docker image registry, it is pulled in layers,
therefore mitigating issues such as connection cuts during pulling and pushing of images.

Many applications are built under a common structure: frontend, backend, and database.
Let's break this down further and understand how we can set this up.

The Frontend

When you open a web application, the page that you see is part of the frontend. Sometimes,
the frontend has the controller (the logical end) and the view layer (the dumb end). The
styling of the layout and content (Read, HTML, and CSS) is the view layer. The content here
is managed by the controller.

The controller influences what is presented in the view layer based on the user's action and/or database changes. Take, for example, an application like Twitter: if someone follows you, your data has changed. The controller will pick up this change and update the view layer with the new number of followers.

The Backend

You might have heard of the term Model-view-controller (MVC). The model sits on the backend side of things in an application. With the earlier example of Twitter, the model does not concern itself with the HTML or its layout. It handles the state of the application: the number of followers and people you are following, the tweets, images, videos, and so on.

This is a summary of what the backend layer includes. The backend mainly deals with the application's logic. This includes the code that is manipulating the database; that means all queries come from the backend. However, requests come from the **frontend**. This happens when a user clicks a button, for example.

You might have also heard of the term API. API is an acronym standing for **Application Program Interface**. This also sits at the backend. APIs expose the internal workings of an application.

This means the API can also be an application's backend or logical layer.

Let's use the Twitter example so that this is clear. Actions such as posting a tweet and searching for tweets can easily be in an API as methods which can be called from any frontend application if the API is made public.

The Docker and `docker-compose` CLIs are actually API calls, for instance when interacting with external resources or content, such as Docker Hub.

The Database

The database contains organized data (information) that is easily accessible, managed, and updated. We have file-based databases and server-based databases.

Server-based databases involve a server process running, accepting requests and reading and writing the database files themselves. The databases could be in the cloud, for example.

Server-based databases are hosted on virtual hosts, mostly on cloud platforms such as Google Cloud Platform and Amazon Web Services. Examples are Amazon RDS and Google Cloud SQL for PostgreSQL.

Obtain server-based databases from the following links:

- `https://aws.amazon.com/rds/postgresql/`
- `https://cloud.google.com/sql/docs/postgres`

In a nutshell, development has always involved building application layers, and shipping has always been a hassle considering the price of the cloud platforms and development and operations (DevOps, for short) involved.

Docker and `docker-compose` help us manage all our application components as a single bundle, which is cheaper, faster, and easier to manage. `docker-compose` helps us coordinate all the application layers through a single file and in very simple definitions.

As we conclude this overview, it is important to know that developers, over time, have coined different stack variations to summarize the frontend, backend, and database structure of their apps. Here's a list of them with their meaning (we will not delve further than this during this course):

- PREN - PostgresDB, React, Express, Node.js
- MEAN - MongoDB, Express, Angular, Node.js
- VPEN - VueJS, PostgresDB, Express, Node.js
- LAMP - Linux, Apache, MySQL, PHP

 It is important to know that applications are structured in this manner to manage separation of concerns.

With the knowledge of application structures, we can get to the `docker-compose` CLI and put this knowledge to work.

Using docker-compose

Using `docker-compose` requires three steps:

1. Build an application's environment as an image using a `Dockerfile`.

2. Use the `docker-compose.yml` file to define the services your app requires to run.

3. Run `docker-compose up` to run the app.

> `docker-compose` is a **command-line interface (CLI)** just like the Docker CLI. Running `docker-compose` gives a list of commands and how to use each.
>
> We went through images in the previous lesson, so step 1 is checked off.
>
> Some `docker-compose` versions are incompatible with some Docker versions.
>
> We'll dwell on step 2 for some time.

Here is the `docker-compose` file:

- One that runs the two images we created in our previous lesson:

```
docker-compose.yml  ✕

1    version: '3'
2
3    services:
4      python:
5        image: python-docker
6      js:
7        image: js-docker
8
```

> Refer the complete code placed at `Code/Lesson-2/example-docker-compose.yml`.
>
> Go to `https://goo.gl/11rwXV` to access the code.

docker-compose first run

1. Create a new directory and name it `py-js`; you can have a different directory name if you prefer.
2. Create a new file in the directory and name it `docker-compose.yml`. Copy the content of the image above or the example shared on example-`docker-compose.yml`.
3. Run the command `docker-compose up` from the directory.

Notice the outputs of running both `js-docker` and `python-docker`. This is also because we have both images built locally from the previous lesson.

If you do not have the images, running `docker-compose up` will result in an error or an attempt to pull it from Docker Hub if it exists online:

```
py-js git:(master) ✗ docker-compose up
Creating network "pyjs_default" with the default driver
Creating pyjs_js_1 ...
Creating pyjs_python_1 ...
Creating pyjs_python_1
Creating pyjs_js_1 ... done
Attaching to pyjs_python_1, pyjs_js_1
python_1  | Hello Docker - PY
js_1      | Hello Docker JS
pyjs_python_1 exited with code 0
pyjs_js_1 exited with code 0
py-js git:(master) ✗
```

- A `docker-compose.yml` that runs **WordPress**. WordPress is a free and open source **content management system (CMS)** based on PHP and MySQL.

Activity 1 — Running WordPress Using docker-compose

To get you conversant with running `docker-compose` commands.

You have been asked to build a WordPress website using `docker-compose`.

1. Create a new directory and name it `sandbox`.

2. Create a new file and name it `docker-compose.yml`. Add the code in `wordpress-docker-compose.yml` or copy the following figure:

```
docker-compose.yml ✕

1    version: '3'
2
3    services:
4      db:
5        image: mysql:latest
6        restart: always
7        environment:
8          MYSQL_ROOT_PASSWORD: hugesecret
9          MYSQL_DATABASE: wordpress
10         MYSQL_USER: test
11         MYSQL_PASSWORD: secret
12
13     wordpress:
14       depends_on:
15         - db
16       image: wordpress:latest
17       ports:
18         - "8000:80"
19       restart: on-failure
20       environment:
21         WORDPRESS_DB_HOST: db:3306
22         WORDPRESS_DB_USER: test
23         WORDPRESS_DB_PASSWORD: secret
24
```

Refer the complete code placed at `Code/Lesson-2/wordpress-docker-compose.yml`.
Go to `https://goo.gl/t7UGvy` to access the code.

Take heed of the indentation in the file. It is advised to use an equal number of tabs and spaces when indenting the lines.

Run `docker-compose up` in the `sandbox` directory:

```
 sandbox git:(master) ✗ docker-compose up
Starting sandbox_db_1 ...
Starting sandbox_db_1 ... done
Starting sandbox_wordpress_1 ...
Starting sandbox_wordpress_1 ... done
Attaching to sandbox_db_1, sandbox_wordpress_1
```

You'll notice that, based on one file, we have an application running. This example is the perfect showcase of the power of `docker-compose`.

Run `docker ps`. You'll see the containers running:

```
CONTAINER ID    IMAGE             COMMAND              CREATED           STATUS          PORTS                   NAMES
4ab2beeaabea    wordpress:latest  "docker-entrypoint..."  About a minute ago  Up About a minute  0.0.0.0:8000->80/tcp   sandbox_wordpress_1
9c55293acb48    mysql:5.7         "docker-entrypoint..."  About a minute ago  Up About a minute  3306/tcp               sandbox_db_1
 ~ 
```

Open your browser and go to the address at: `http://0.0.0.0:8000/`. We'll have the WordPress website set up ready.

Proceed with the set up and, in an instant, you have a WordPress site up and ready.

The docker-compose file: docker-compose.yml

`docker-compose.yml` is a YAML file. It defines services, networks, and volumes.

Services are application container definitions that include all components that relate to an application, for example, **DB, frontend,** or **backend.** What really weighs in when defining services is the components, which are networks, volumes, and environment variables.

The first line of any `docker-compose.yml` defines the version of the `docker-compose` file format.

By running `docker -v`, you can tell which Docker version is running and thus know which version to put on the first line of the file.

For `docker-compose` file format 1.0, the first line was not necessary. Each `docker-compose` file introduced a new configuration or deprecated an earlier one.

We will use version 3.3 and the program should be compatible with version 3.0 and above.

Make sure everyone is running version 3 and at least a Docker that's 1.13.0+.

Next up is services. Let's use this simplified skeleton:

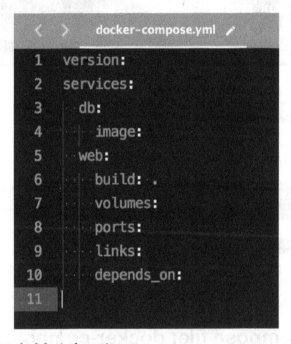

```
1   version:
2   services:
3     db:
4       image:
5     web:
6       build: .
7       volumes:
8       ports:
9       links:
10      depends_on:
11
```

 Take heed of the indentation.

In the above example, we have two services, that is, db and web. These two are indented just once.

The next lines after defining the services defines the image or the Dockerfile from which the image is to be built.

Line 4 will specify the image from which the db service container will run from. We earlier mentioned a number of stacks; the db image can be any of the server-based databases.

> To confirm whether a stack you want to use exists, run the following:
> `docker search <image or name of your preferred stack>`
> (for example, `docker search mongo` or `docker search postgres`).

Line 6 explains that the web services image will be built from the Dockerfile in the location (.) relative to the `docker-compose.yml`.

We can also define the name of the Dockerfile in line 6. `docker-compose` will search for the file with a name as listed, for example, in the `docker-compose.yml`:

```
Line 5| web:
          build: Dockerfile
          volumes:
```

Lines 7 to 10 gives more definition to the web services.

As evidenced in the `docker-compose.yml` we used to build and run WordPress, there are two services: db and wordpress. In the output of `docker ps`, these are the container names: `sandbox_wordpress_1` and `sandbox_db_1`.
The first word before the underscore signifies the name of the directory holding the `docker-compose.yml`. The second word in that container name is the service name, as defined in `docker-compose.yml`.

We'll go into more context in the following topic.

The docker-compose CLI

As soon as `docker-compose` is installed, I mentioned that you expect a list of options when you run `docker-compose`. Run `docker-compose -v`.

> These two commands, `docker-compose` and `docker-compose -v`, are the only ones that can be ran from whichever working directory is open on your terminal command line or Git bash.

Otherwise, the other options in `docker-compose` are only run in the presence of the `docker-compose.yml` file.

Let's dig deep into the common commands: `docker-compose build`.

This command builds images referenced in the `docker-compose line: (build: .)` in the template `docker-compose.ym`.

Building images can also be achieved through the command `docker-compose up`. Take note that this doesn't happen unless the image has not been built yet, or there has been a recent change that affects the container to be run.

 This command will also work for the WordPress example, even though both services run from images in the Docker registry and not Dockerfiles within the directory. This would be **pulling** an image and **not building** because we build from a Dockerfile.

This command lists the services as configured in the `docker-compose.yml`:

- `docker-compose config --services`

This command lists the images used by the created containers:

- `docker-compose images`

This command lists the logs from the services:

- `docker-compose logs`

`docker-compose logs <service>` lists the logs of a specific service, for example, `docker-compose logs db`.

This command lists the containers running based on the `docker-compose`:

- `docker-compose ps`

Note that in most cases, there is a difference between the results of `docker-compose ps` and `docker ps`. Containers that were not running in the context of `docker-compose` will not be displayed by the command `docker-compose ps`.

This command builds, creates, recreates, and runs services:

- `docker-compose up`

 When running `docker-compose up`, if one service exits, the entire command exits.

Running `docker-compose up -d` is running `docker-compose up` in detached mode. That is, the command will be running in the background.

Activity 2 — Analyzing the docker- compose CLI

To get you conversant with the `docker-compose` CLI.

You have been asked to demonstrate the difference in changes resulting from running two containers.

While still within the directory with the WordPress `docker-compose.yml`-- in my case, sandbox -- run the commands of *Activity B-1*, then the following commands:

```
docker-compose up -d
docker-compose stop
docker-compose rm
docker-compose start
docker-compose up -d
docker-compose stop
docker-compose start
```

Managing Multiple Containers and Distributed Application Bundles

This is the `docker-compose.yml` for running a Django application. A similar application can be found in the `docker-compose` documentation under the Django example.

Download the Django example from: `https://docs.docker.com/compose/django/`:

```
docker-compose.yml ✕
1    version: '3'
2
3    services:
4    ··db:
5    ··|··image: postgres:latest
6    ··web:
7    ··|··build: .
8    ··|··command: python3 manage.py runserver 0.0.0.0:8000
9    ··|··volumes:
10   ··|··|··- .:/django_docker
11   ··|··ports:
12   ··|··|··- "8000:8000"
13   ··|··depends_on:
14   ··|··|··- db
```

Refer the complete code placed at `Code/Lesson-2/django-docker-compose.yml`.

Go to `https://goo.gl/H624J1` to access the code.

Improve a Docker Workflow

To give more context on how `docker-compose` is involved and how it improves a Docker workflow.

1. Create a new directory and name it `django_docker`.

2. In the `django-docker` directory, create a new `docker-compose.yml` and add the information in the figure above, or in the `django-docker-compose.yml` script provided.

3. Create a new Dockerfile and add the content in the Dockerfile script provided.

4. Create a requirements file; simply copy the `django-requirements.txt` file provided.

5. Run `docker-compose` up and observe the logs.

Notice that we are able to spin up both containers with one simple command, docker-compose up.

 No prior experience with Django is needed; this is for basic demo purposes. `Code/Lesson-2/django-requirements.txt`.

The Django Compose File Broken Down

First things first, how many services does this file have? Yes, two: `db` and `web`. The service `db` is based on the Postgres image. The service web is built from the Dockerfile in the same directory that contains this `docker-compose.yml`.

Without the `docker-compose` file, the `db` service container would have otherwise been run in this way:

```
~ docker run postgres
The files belonging to this database system will be owned by user "postgres".
This user must also own the server process.

The database cluster will be initialized with locale "en_US.utf8".
The default database encoding has accordingly been set to "UTF8".
The default text search configuration will be set to "english".

Data page checksums are disabled.
```

This command is translated to the following:

```
3    services:
4      db:
5        image: postgres:latest
```

Open another tab or window in the terminal and run `docker ps`. You'll see the container running.

On the other hand, the `web` service container as per the example would be run in the following steps:

```
django_docker docker run -p 8000:8000 -v `pwd`:/django_docker django-web python3 manage.py runserver 0.0.0.0:8000
```

The second command, broken down, is in the following format:

```
docker run (the command)
        -p  shows the <workstation-port>:<container-port>
        (8000:8000)
        -v: shows the <present-working-directory>  `pwd`
        <working-directory-in-container>  (:/django_docker)
        <docker image> (django-web)
        <command-to-run-when-the-container-starts> (python3
        manage.py runserver 0.0.0.0.8000)
```

Therefore, the aforementioned command is translated to the following:

```
 6   web:
 7     build: .
 8     command: python3 manage.py runserver 0.0.0.0:8000
 9     volumes:
10       - .:/django_docker
11     ports:
12       - "8000:8000"
```

One advantage of using `docker-compose.yml` is that instead of running the commands in the terminal again and again, you have one command to run as many containers as you've included in the file.

We did not cover volumes and ports in the last lesson. I'll take time to help us understand this.

Endure Data Using Volumes

Volumes are used to persist data generated and used by Docker containers.

 Volumes persist any update to a local file or script. This makes an equal change on the container side.

In this case, the command is the following:

```
django_docker docker run -p 8000:8000 -v `pwd`:/django_docker django-web python3 manage.py runserver 0.0.0.0:8000
```

In the docker run options, which comes after the main command:

```
-v .:/django_docker
```

This is in the `docker-compose.yml` file.

```
 9    volumes:
10      - .:/django_docker
```

 As long as volumes is defined in the `docker-compose` file, when a local change is made, such as a file update, the changes will be automatically synced to the files in the container(s).

```
django_docker docker run -p 8000:8000 -v `pwd`:/django_docker django-web python3 manage.py runserver 0.0.0.0:8000
```

Ports

Django, as other web servers do, runs on specific ports. The Dockerfile used to build the Django image has a similar command to this: EXPOSE 8000.
This port remains open when the container is run and is open for connection.

In the Django Dockerfile, we defined our port as 8000 and prefixed the number with an address (0.0.0.0):

```
8        command: python3 manage.py runserver 0.0.0.0:8000
```

The number 0.0.0.0 defines the host address running the container.

> The address tells docker-compose to run the container on our machine or, in short, localhost. If we were to skip the address and just expose the port, our set up would have unexpected results like a blank page.

Consider the following line in the docker run options:

```
-p 8000:8000
```

```
django_docker docker run -p 8000:8000 -v `pwd`:/django_docker django-web python3 manage.py runserver 0.0.0.0:8000
```

And the following lines in the docker-compose.yml:

```
11        ports:
12          - "8000:8000"
```

The docker-compose port format maps the local workstation port to container port. The format is as follows:

```
-p <workstation-port>:<container-port>
```

This allows us from our local machine to access the port 8000 which was mapped from the container port.

There's one option at the end, depends_on, that is specific to docker-compose.yml. The depends_on specifies the order in which the containers are spun up as soon as we run docker-compose run.

In our case, the depends_on option is under the web service. This means that the web service container depends on the db service container:

```
13          ....depends_on:
14          ......- db
```

Activity 3 — Running the docker-compose File

To get you conversant with the docker-compose syntax and commands.

You have been asked to build and run a simple Python application which exposes port 5000 from the image josephmuli/flask-app. Define a docker-compose file and extend the Postgres image as the database. Make sure the database relates to the application.

1. I have prebuilt an image with the name josephmuli/flask-app. Extend this image in your docker-compose.yml file.
2. Make sure to write a version 3 docker-compose and define the two services.
3. Run the application on port 5000.
4. Open your browser and check the listening port.

Networking with docker-compose

By default, docker-compose sets up a single network for your application(s) where each container can reach and discover other containers.

The network is given a name based on the name of the directory it lives in. Thus, if your directory is called py_docker, when your run docker-compose up, the network created is called py_docker_default.

We mentioned ports in the previous topic, when creating the WordPress container. To explain networking better, we'll use the `docker-compose.yml` used to spin up a WordPress application:

```
docker-compose.yml ✕
1    version: '3'
2
3    services:
4      db:
5        image: mysql:latest
6        restart: always
7        environment:
8          MYSQL_ROOT_PASSWORD: hugesecret
9          MYSQL_DATABASE: wordpress
10         MYSQL_USER: test
11         MYSQL_PASSWORD: secret
12
13     wordpress:
14       depends_on:
15         - db
16       image: wordpress:latest
17       ports:
18         - "8000:80"
19       restart: on-failure
20       environment:
21         WORDPRESS_DB_HOST: db:3306
22         WORDPRESS_DB_USER: test
23         WORDPRESS_DB_PASSWORD: secret
24
```

In this file, we have two services: `db` and `wordpress`.

In the WordPress service, we have the `ports` option mapping port `80` to port `8000`. No wonder, the WordPress app runs on `0.0.0.0:8000` on our browsers.

The ports option is not in the `db` service. However, if you go to the `docker hub page for mysql`, you'll notice that port `3306` is exposed. This is the standard port for MySQL. You can obtain more information on MySQL from: `https://hub.docker.com/r/library/mysql`.

 We don't have port mapping for DB because we don't necessarily need the port mapped to our computer; instead, we want the WordPress app mapped to the DB for communication.

We don't have port mapping for `db` because we don't necessarily need the port mapped to our local workstation or computer.

We only need it to be exposed in the container environment and thus it can be connected from the web service as in line 23: `WORDPRESS_DB_HOST: db:3306`.

> In the `docker-compose` file, this is how you connect one container to another:
>
> 1. Note the port exposed by the image(s) you want to connect.
> 2. Reference the container under the service that is connecting to it; in our case, the db service is connected to by the WordPress service.
>   Since we named the service db, we reference this connection as `db:3306`.
>   Therefore, the format is `<service>:<port exposed by that service>`.

Run the WordPress Containers

To give more context on how containers are connected, sync, and communicate.

In the compose file, did you notice the restart option? The available values for this option are as follows:

- no
- always
- on-failure
- unless-stopped

```
3    services:
4        db:
5            image: mysql:latest
6            restart: always
```

If it is not specified, the default is no. This means that the container will not be restarted under any circumstance. However, the db service here has been specified as restart: always, so the container always restarts.

Let's look at the Django example and see how networking works out there. This is the docker-compose.yml:

```
 docker-compose.yml  ✕

1     version: '3'
2
3     services:
4       db:
5         image: postgres:latest
6       web:
7         build: .
8         command: python3 manage.py runserver 0.0.0.0:8000
9         volumes:
10          - .:/django_docker
11        ports:
12          - "8000:8000"
13        depends_on:
14          - db
15
```

Immediately, you might not see the networking section present in the WordPress site. Here's a snippet:

```
DATABASES = {
    'default': {
        'ENGINE': 'django.db.backends.postgresql',
        'NAME': 'postgres',
        'USER': 'postgres',
        'HOST': 'db',
        'PORT': 5432,
    }
}
```

The question here is, how did we know that the name and user is postgres, the HOST is db, and the port is 5432?

These are the default values set in the postgres image and containers we run.

For more clarity, you can take a look at this line, in the official Postgres Docker library:

You can obtain a Postgres Docker sample from GitHub at: `https://github.com/docker-library/postgres/blob/master/10/docker-entrypoint.sh#L101`.

```
101            file_env 'POSTGRES_USER' 'postgres'
102            file_env 'POSTGRES_DB' "$POSTGRES_USER"
103
```

As earlier explained, the Host is DB because the service name is db that is created by running the `postgres` image.

You can obtain a Postgres Docker example from GitHub at: `https://github.com/docker-library/postgres/blob/master/10/Dockerfile#L132`:

We go our port number at: `https://github.com/docker-library/postgres/blob/master/10/Dockerfile#L132`:

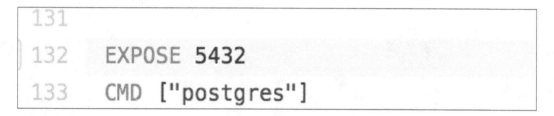

```
131
132    EXPOSE 5432
133    CMD ["postgres"]
```

Indirectly, it proves why the `settings.py` was configured in that manner.

Summary

In this lesson, we have done the following:

- Discussed and displayed a multi-container setup
- Walked through `docker-compose` commands to build and run multiple containers in a parallel manner
- Gained a high-level understanding of networking containers and how data is persisted in a container from local machines
- Built and run applications without even setting them up, via Docker Hub

3

Orchestration and Delivery

The main motivation behind creating a cluster of Docker hosts is designing for high availability. Most, if not all, clustering and orchestration tools, such as Docker Swarm and Kubernetes, take advantage of clustering by creating a master-slave kind of relationship. This ensures that there is always a node to fall back to in case any one node goes down in the environment. While deploying a cluster to a cloud provider, there are a couple of technologies you can leverage to ensure that your environment is highly available, for example Consul, and also take advantage of the native fault-tolerant design of the cloud by deploying masters and nodes in separate availability zones.

Lesson Objectives

By the end of this lesson, you will be able to:

- Obtain an overview of the Docker Swarm mode
- Use Docker engine to create a swarm of Docker engines
- Manage services and applications in a swarm
- Scale services up and down to handle more requests on your application
- Load balance a Docker Swarm deployment
- Secure Docker containers and deployments

Orchestration

Running containers on our local environment is easy and does not require a lot of our effort; when it comes to the cloud, we need a different kind of mindset and tools to aid us in achieving this. Our environment should be highly available, fault tolerant, and easily scalable. This process of coordinating resources and/or containers, resulting in a consolidated workflow, is orchestration.

First, let's get familiarized with some of the terms used when it comes to orchestration:

- docker-engine: This refers to the Docker bundle or installation we currently have on our computers
- docker-machine: A tool that helps us install Docker on virtual hosts
- Virtual hosts: These are virtual servers that run under physical hosts
- docker-swarm: A clustering tool for Docker
- docker host: A host or server that has Docker set up or installed
- Node: A Docker host that is connected to a swarm cluster
- Cluster: A group of Docker hosts or nodes
- Replica: A duplicate or number of duplicates of an instance
- Task: A defined operation to be run on nodes
- Service: A group of tasks

Here are the most common terms throughout the lesson:
- `docker-engine`: running Docker on our computers;
- `docker-machine`: A tool or CLI that helps us install Docker
- `Virtual hosts`: A host or server running on a physical host.
- `docker-swarm`: A clustering tool for Docker
- `Docker host`: Any server or host running Docker
- `Node`: This refers to any host bound to a swarm cluster.
- `Cluster`: A group of managed and controlled hosts.
- `Replica`: A duplicate of other running hosts for various tasks
- `Task`: Operations like install, upgrade, or remove.
- `Service`: Multiple tasks define a service.

Now that we are at least conversant with the terms above, we are ready to implement a Docker Swarm orchestration flow using `docker-machine`.

An Overview of Docker Swarm

Docker Swarm is a clustering tool for Docker containers. It allows you to establish and manage a cluster of Docker nodes as a single virtual system. This means we get to run Docker on multiple hosts on our computers.

We control the swarm cluster through a manager which primarily **handles** and **controls** containers. With the swarm manager, you can create a primary manager instance and multiple **replica** instances in case the primary fails. This means you can have more than one manager in a swarm!

A swarm is created from a manager node, and other Docker machines join the cluster, either as worker nodes or manager nodes.

Clustering is important because it creates a group of cooperating systems that provide redundancy, creating a fault-tolerant environment. For example, if one or more of the nodes goes down, Docker Swarm will fail over to another working node.

The Swarm manager carries out the following roles:

- Accepts `docker` commands
- Executes commands against the cluster
- Supports high availability; deploys a primary and secondary instance which can take over in the event of the primary instance going down

Docker Swarm uses scheduling to optimize resources and ensure efficiency in the environment. It assigns containers to the most appropriate nodes. This means Docker Swarm will assign containers to the most healthy node.

 Remember, a node is a host running Docker, not a container.

Swarm can be configured to use any of the following scheduling strategies:

- **Random**: Deploys a new container to a random node.
- **Spread**: Swarm deploys a new container to the node with the least number of containers.
- **Binpack**: The binpack strategy involves deploying a new container to the node with the highest number of containers.

You can download VirtualBox at: `https://www.virtualbox.org/wiki/Downloads`:

Download VirtualBox

Here, you will find links to VirtualBox binaries and its source code.

VirtualBox binaries

By downloading, you agree to the terms and conditions of the respective license.

If you're looking for the VirtualBox 5.1.30 packages, see VirtualBox 5.1 builds. Consider upgrading.

- **VirtualBox 5.2.2 platform packages**. The binaries are released under the terms of the GPL version 2.
    - ⇨Windows hosts
    - ⇨OS X hosts
    - Linux distributions
    - ⇨Solaris hosts

 To simulate a Docker Swarm cluster, we need to install a hypervisor (a hypervisor type 2 is a virtual machine manager that is installed as a software application on an existing operating system) locally, in this case VirtualBox, that will allow us to create multiple hosts running Docker locally via `docker-machine` and then add them to the swarm cluster. While deploying to a cloud vendor, this is achieved using their compute service, for instance EC2 on AWS.

For Windows operating systems, select your OS distribution and you should get a download immediately. Run the executable and install VirtualBox.

Using Docker Engine to Create a Swarm

Before we create our swarm, let's get a quick overview of the `docker-machine cli`. Typing `docker-machine` on your terminal should give you this output:

```
→ Lesson-3 docker-machine
Usage: docker-machine [OPTIONS] COMMAND [arg...]

Create and manage machines running Docker.

Version: 0.13.0, build 9ba6da9

Author:
  Docker Machine Contributors - <https://github.com/docker/machine>

Options:
  --debug, -D                                               Enable debug mode
  --storage-path, -s "/Users/josephmuli/.docker/machine"    Configures storage path [$MACHINE_STORAGE_PATH]
  --tls-ca-cert                                             CA to verify remotes against [$MACHINE_TLS_CA_CERT]
  --tls-ca-key                                             Private key to generate certificates [$MACHINE_TLS_CA_KEY]
  --tls-client-cert                                         Client cert to use for TLS [$MACHINE_TLS_CLIENT_CERT]
  --tls-client-key                                         Private key used in client TLS auth [$MACHINE_TLS_CLIENT_KEY]
  --github-api-token                                       Token to use for requests to the Github API [$MACHINE_GITHUB_
API_TOKEN]
  --native-ssh                                             Use the native (Go-based) SSH implementation. [$MACHINE_NATIV
E_SSH]
  --bugsnag-api-token                                       BugSnag API token for crash reporting [$MACHINE_BUGSNAG_API_T
OKEN]
  --help, -h                                               show help
  --version, -v                                             print the version
```

Just below that, we have our list of commands:

```
Commands:
  active            Print which machine is active
  config            Print the connection config for machine
  create            Create a machine
  env               Display the commands to set up the environment for the Docker client
  inspect           Inspect information about a machine
  ip                Get the IP address of a machine
  kill              Kill a machine
  ls                List machines
  provision         Re-provision existing machines
  regenerate-certs  Regenerate TLS Certificates for a machine
  restart           Restart a machine
  rm                Remove a machine
  ssh               Log into or run a command on a machine with SSH.
  scp               Copy files between machines
  mount             Mount or unmount a directory from a machine with SSHFS.
  start             Start a machine
  status            Get the status of a machine
  stop              Stop a machine
  upgrade           Upgrade a machine to the latest version of Docker
  url               Get the URL of a machine
  version           Show the Docker Machine version or a machine docker version
  help              Shows a list of commands or help for one command
```

Remember to always use the `help` option when you need to clarify something, that is, `docker-machine stop --help`

To create our first Docker Swarm cluster, we are going to use `docker-machine` to create our manager and worker nodes first.

Before creating the first machine, a quick overview of our objectives gives us the following: we are going to have four docker-machines, one manager, and three workers; they are all running on VirtualBox, thus there are four virtual machines.

Creating Docker Machines

This command is used to create a new virtual Docker host:

```
docker-machine create --driver <driver> <machine_name>
```

This means our Docker host will be running on VirtualBox, but managed and controlled by `docker-machine`. The `--driver` option specifies the driver to create the machine with. In this case, our driver is VirtualBox.

Our command will be `docker-machine create --driver virtualbox manager1`.

We require the driver in the command because that is our host's foundation, meaning our `manager1` machine will be running on VirtualBox as a virtual host. There are multiple drivers available from different vendors, but this is the best one for demo purposes.

```
→ Lesson-3 docker-machine create --driver virtualbox manager1
Running pre-create checks...
Creating machine...
(manager1) Copying /Users/josephmuli/.docker/machine/cache/boot2docker.iso to /Users/josephmuli/.docker/machine/machines/mana
ger1/boot2docker.iso...
(manager1) Creating VirtualBox VM...
(manager1) Creating SSH key...
(manager1) Starting the VM...
(manager1) Check network to re-create if needed...
(manager1) Waiting for an IP...
Waiting for machine to be running, this may take a few minutes...
Detecting operating system of created instance...
Waiting for SSH to be available...
Detecting the provisioner...
Provisioning with boot2docker...
Copying certs to the local machine directory...
Copying certs to the remote machine...
Setting Docker configuration on the remote daemon...
Checking connection to Docker...
Docker is up and running!
To see how to connect your Docker Client to the Docker Engine running on this virtual machine, run: docker-machine env manage
r1
→ Lesson-3 
```

Listing Created Machines

This command will provide a listing of all the Docker Machines currently on your host and more information such as the state, driver, and so on of the machine:

`docker-machine ls`

```
→ Lesson-3 docker-machine ls
NAME        ACTIVE    DRIVER      STATE     URL                           SWARM    DOCKER        ERRORS
manager1    -         virtualbox  Running   tcp://192.168.99.100:2376              v17.09.1-ce
→ Lesson-3 
```

 Listing our machine is very important as it gives us an update of our machine status. We don't really get notified of errors, which at times could build up to a fateful event. Before doing some work on a machine, this will give a brief overview. A more detailed check can be run through the `docker-machine status` command.

Worker Machine Creation

We will follow the same process to create three worker machines for our swarm cluster, in other words, running `docker-machine create --driver virtualbox <machine_name>` three times, passing `worker1`, `worker2`, and `worker3` as the value for `<machine_name>` on each subsequent run:

```
→ Lesson-3 docker-machine create --driver virtualbox worker1
Running pre-create checks...
Creating machine...
(worker1) Copying /Users/josephmuli/.docker/machine/cache/boot2docker.iso to /Users/josephmuli/.docker/machine/machines/worke
r1/boot2docker.iso...
(worker1) Creating VirtualBox VM...
(worker1) Creating SSH key...
(worker1) Starting the VM...
(worker1) Check network to re-create if needed...
(worker1) Waiting for an IP...
Waiting for machine to be running, this may take a few minutes...
Detecting operating system of created instance...
Waiting for SSH to be available...
Detecting the provisioner...
Provisioning with boot2docker...
Copying certs to the local machine directory...
Copying certs to the remote machine...
Setting Docker configuration on the remote daemon...
Checking connection to Docker...
Docker is up and running!
To see how to connect your Docker Client to the Docker Engine running on this virtual machine, run: docker-machine env worker
1
→ Lesson-3 
```

```
→ Lesson-3 docker-machine create --driver virtualbox worker2
Running pre-create checks...
Creating machine...
(worker2) Copying /Users/josephmuli/.docker/machine/cache/boot2docker.iso to /Users/josephmuli/.docker/machine/machines/worke
r2/boot2docker.iso...
(worker2) Creating VirtualBox VM...
(worker2) Creating SSH key...
(worker2) Starting the VM...
(worker2) Check network to re-create if needed...
(worker2) Waiting for an IP...
Waiting for machine to be running, this may take a few minutes...
Detecting operating system of created instance...
Waiting for SSH to be available...
Detecting the provisioner...
Provisioning with boot2docker...
Copying certs to the local machine directory...
Copying certs to the remote machine...
Setting Docker configuration on the remote daemon...
Checking connection to Docker...
Docker is up and running!
To see how to connect your Docker Client to the Docker Engine running on this virtual machine, run: docker-machine env worker
2
```

Finally, the last worker node will be displayed as follows:

```
→ Lesson-3 docker-machine create --driver virtualbox worker3
Running pre-create checks...
Creating machine...
(worker3) Copying /Users/josephmuli/.docker/machine/cache/boot2docker.iso to /Users/josephmuli/.docker/machine/machines/worke
r3/boot2docker.iso...
(worker3) Creating VirtualBox VM...
(worker3) Creating SSH key...
(worker3) Starting the VM...
(worker3) Check network to re-create if needed...
(worker3) Waiting for an IP...
Waiting for machine to be running, this may take a few minutes...
Detecting operating system of created instance...
Waiting for SSH to be available...
Detecting the provisioner...
Provisioning with boot2docker...
Copying certs to the local machine directory...
Copying certs to the remote machine...
Setting Docker configuration on the remote daemon...
Checking connection to Docker...
Docker is up and running!
To see how to connect your Docker Client to the Docker Engine running on this virtual machine, run: docker-machine env worker
3
```

After doing so, run `docker-machine ls` and if the creation was successful, you will see an output similar to the following:

```
→ Lesson-3 docker-machine ls
NAME       ACTIVE   DRIVER       STATE     URL                           SWARM   DOCKER       ERRORS
manager1   -        virtualbox   Running   tcp://192.168.99.100:2376             v17.09.1-ce
worker1    -        virtualbox   Running   tcp://192.168.99.101:2376             v17.09.1-ce
worker2    -        virtualbox   Running   tcp://192.168.99.102:2376             v17.09.1-ce
worker3    -        virtualbox   Running   tcp://192.168.99.103:2376             v17.09.1-ce
→ Lesson-3
```

 Naming the machines according to their purpose helps us avoid unexpected calls to the wrong hosts.

Initializing our Swarm

Now that we have our machines running, it's time to create our swarm. This will be done through the manager node, manager1. The following are the steps we will take to achieve a full-fledged swarm:

1. Connect to the manager node.
2. Declare the manager1 node as the manager and advertise its address.
3. Get the invite address for nodes to join the swarm.

We will be using `ssh` for our connection. `ssh` is a secure network protocol used to access or connect to hosts or servers.

 Docker Machines are controlled via the `docker-machine cli`. Docker Swarm runs as a service that bonds all the Docker Machines and unifies them under a manager machine, or node. This doesn't mean the machines in a swarm cluster are equal or similar in any way, they could all be running different services or operations, for example, a database host and a web server. Docker Swarm comes in to help orchestrate the hosts.

This command is used to get the IP address of one or more Docker machines:

```
docker-machine ip <machine_names>
```

This command is used to get the IP address of one or more Docker machines. The `<machine_name>` is the name or names of the machines whose IP addresses we need. In our case, we will use it to get the IP address of the `manager1` node as we will need it when initializing swarm mode:

```
➜  Lesson-3 docker-machine ip manager1
192.168.99.100
➜  Lesson-3 
```

Connecting to a Machine

This command is used to log into a machine using `SSH`:

```
docker-machine ssh <machine_name>
```

After a successful connection to our `manager1`, we should get an output that looks like the following:

```
→  Lesson-3 docker-machine ssh manager1
                        ##         .
                  ## ## ##        ==
               ## ## ## ## ##    ===
           /""""""""""""""""\___/ ===
      ~~~ {~~ ~~~~ ~~~ ~~~~ ~~ ~ /  ===- ~~~
           _____ o          __/
             \    \        __/
              _____/
 _                 _   ____     _            _
| |__   ___   ___ | |_|___ \ __| | ___   ___| | _____ _ __
| '_ \ / _ \ / _ \| __| __) / _` |/ _ \ / __| |/ / _ \ '__|
| |_) | (_) | (_) | |_ / __/ (_| | (_) | (__|   <  __/ |
|_.__/ \___/ \___/ \__|_____,_|\___/ \___|_|\_\___|_|
Boot2Docker version 17.09.1-ce, build HEAD : e7de9ae - Fri Dec  8 19:41:36 UTC 2017
Docker version 17.09.1-ce, build 19e2cf6
docker@manager1:~$ █
```

 Using the `ssh protocol` on cloud vendors will require authentication and/or authorization through usernames and passwords or `ssh keys`. We will not be going deeper into this because this is a demo.

Initializing Swarm Mode

Here is the command to initialize the swarm mode:

```
docker swarm init --advertise-addr <MANAGER_IP>
```

Let's run this command inside the manager node to initialize a swarm. The `advertise-addr` option is used to specify the address that will be advertised to other members of the swarm for API access and networking.

In this case, its value is the `manager IP address` whose value we got from running the `docker-machine ip manager1` earlier:

 We mentioned earlier that Docker Swarm is a service that bonds and orchestrates all machines through a manager node. For this to happen, Docker Swarm lets us advertise the cluster through the address of the manager, by including `advertise-addr` in the `docker swarm init` command.

```
docker@manager1:~$ docker swarm init --advertise-addr 192.168.99.100
Swarm initialized: current node (ekckmr7qf8v5qj4v6ojmro2a3) is now a manager.

To add a worker to this swarm, run the following command:

    docker swarm join --token SWMTKN-1-1xk4mxwd7afjohspramr3qkbmp93es9pxl52vjitvbyoy4nmy4-71gjzypznjdkmkb631nov4yli 192.168.99.100:2377

To add a manager to this swarm, run 'docker swarm join-token manager' and follow the instructions.

docker@manager1:~$
```

The output of running the command shows us that our node is now a manager!

Notice we also have two commands: one should allow us to invite other nodes to the cluster and the other to add another manager to the cluster.

 When designing for high availability, it is recommended to have more than one manager node that will take over in the case of a failure on the primary manager node.

 Ensure you save two commands listed in the output as they will be useful in adding other hosts in the swarm.

Adding Workers to our Swarm

This command is used to add swarm workers:

```
docker swarm join --token <provided_token> <manager_ip>:<port>
```

Before we can add our workers to the swarm, we will need to connect to them, through `ssh`.

We achieve this by running `docker-machine ssh <node_name>` and then running the invite command we got from the `manager1 node`.

 The `docker-machine` command can be run from any directory and will always work with the created machines.

First, we will exit the manager node, using the `exit` command:

```
docker@manager1:~$ exit
→ Lesson-3
```

Then, we connect to a worker node via `ssh`:

```
→ Lesson-3 docker-machine ssh testworker
                      ##         .
                ## ## ##        ==
             ## ## ## ## ##    ===
         /""""""""""""""""\___/ ===
    ~~~ {~~ ~~~~ ~~~ ~~~~ ~~~ ~ /  ===- ~~~
         _____ o          __/
          \    \        __/
           _____/
```

Finally, we add the node to the cluster:

```
→ Lesson-3 docker-machine ssh testworker
                        ##         .
                  ## ## ##        ==
               ## ## ## ##       ===
           /""""""""""""""""\___/ ===
      ~~~ {~~ ~~~~ ~~~ ~~~~ ~~ ~ /  ===- ~~~
           _____ o          __/
             \    \        __/
              _____/


  ____  ____  ____ _____ ___ ____   ____  ____ _  _ ____ ____
 |  _ \/ _  \/ _  |_  _  |__ )/___ \ |  _ \/ _  | |/ /|  __|  _ \
 | |_| | | | | | | | | | |  _ < ____) || |_| | | | |   / |  __| |_| |
 |____/\___/ \___/  |_|  |___/|_____/ |____/\___/ |_|\_\|____|____/

Boot2Docker version 17.09.1-ce, build HEAD : e7de9ae - Fri Dec  8 19:41:36 UTC 2017
Docker version 17.09.1-ce, build 19e2cf6
docker@testworker:~$ docker swarm join --token SWMTKN-1-1xk4mxwd7afjohspramr3qkbmp93es9pxl52vjitvbyoy4nmy4-71gjzypznjdkmkb631nov4yli 192.168.99.100:2377
This node joined a swarm as a worker.
docker@testworker:~$ 
```

Viewing a Cluster's Status

We use this command to view the status of our cluster:

```
docker node ls
```

We use this command to view the status of our cluster. This command is run on the manager node and displays all the nodes in our cluster and their status and availability. Running this on our manager node shows output similar to that of the following:

```
docker@manager1:~$ docker node ls
ID                            HOSTNAME     STATUS    AVAILABILITY    MANAGER STATUS
r4ov0ovzh1l1cllf8aeqxpsac     dbworker     Down      Active
ekckmr7qf8v5qj4v6ojmro2a3 *   manager1     Ready     Active          Leader
j97cjg16g4gwgpxz48dvg6h5o     worker1      Ready     Active
sbmurdxvyk7t3jqzncr9xrl5s     worker2      Ready     Active
docker@manager1:~$ 
```

Activity 1 — Adding Nodes to a Cluster

Ensure you have a manager node and the node invite command.

To get you conversant with ssh and cluster management.

You have been asked to connect to at least two nodes and add them to the cluster.

1. Ssh into your first node:

```
docker@manager1:~$ exit
→ Lesson-3 docker-machine ssh worker1
                        ##
                 ## ## ##           .
              ## ## ## ## ##       __
           /""""""""""""""""\___/ ===
      ~~~ {~~ ~~~~ ~~~ ~~~~ ~~ ~ /  ===- ~~~
           _____ o          __/
            \    \        __/
             _____/
 __        __  ___   ____   _  _____ ____  _
 \ \      / / / _ \ |  _ \ | |/ / __|  _ \/ |
  \ \ /\ / / | | | || |_) || ' /|  _|| |_) | |
   \ V  V /  | |_| ||  _ < | . \| |___|  _ <| |
    \_/\_/    \___/ |_| \_\|_|\_\____|_| \_\_|
Boot2Docker version 17.09.1-ce, build HEAD : e7de9ae - Fri Dec  8 19:41:36 UTC 2017
Docker version 17.09.1-ce, build 19e2cf6
docker@worker1:~$
```

2. Run the invite command on the node to join the cluster. Remember, we got this command when we first initialized our manager node:

```
docker@worker1:~$ docker swarm join --token SWMTKN-1-1xk4mxwd7afjohspramr3qkbmp93es9pxl52vjitvbyoy4rmy4-71gjzypznjdkmkb631nov4yli 192.168.99.100:2377
This node joined a swarm as a worker.
docker@worker1:~$
```

3. Exit the node, ssh into another, and run the command:

```
docker@worker1:~$ exit
→ Lesson-3 docker-machine ssh worker2
                        ##
                 ## ## ##
              ## ## ## ## ##
           /""""""""""""""""\___/ ===
      ~~~ {~~ ~~~~ ~~~ ~~~~ ~~ ~ /  ===- ~~~
           _____ o          __/
            \    \        __/
             _____/
 __        __  ___   ____   _  _____ ____  ____
 \ \      / / / _ \ |  _ \ | |/ / __|  _ \|___ \
  \ \ /\ / / | | | || |_) || ' /|  _|| |_) | __) |
   \ V  V /  | |_| ||  _ < | . \| |___|  _ < / __/
    \_/\_/    \___/ |_| \_\|_|\_\____|_| _____|
Boot2Docker version 17.09.1-ce, build HEAD : e7de9ae - Fri Dec  8 19:41:36 UTC 2017
Docker version 17.09.1-ce, build 19e2cf6
docker@worker2:~$ docker swarm join --token SWMTKN-1-1xk4mxwd7afjohspramr3qkbmp93es9pxl52vjitvbyoy4rmy4-71gjzypznjdkmkb631nov4yli 192.168.99.100:2377
This node joined a swarm as a worker.
docker@worker2:~$
```

4. Ssh into the manager node to check the cluster status through `docker node ls`:

```
→ Lesson-3 docker-machine ssh manager1
                        ##         .
                  ## ## ##        ==
               ## ## ## ## ##    ===
           /""""""""""""""""""\___/ ===
      ~~~ {~~ ~~~~ ~~~ ~~~~ ~~ ~ /  ===- ~~~
           _____ o           __/
             \    \         __/
              _____/


Boot2Docker version 17.09.1-ce, build HEAD : e7de9ae - Fri Dec  8 19:41:36 UTC 2017
Docker version 17.09.1-ce, build 19e2cf6
docker@manager1:~$ docker node ls
ID                             HOSTNAME      STATUS    AVAILABILITY    MANAGER STATUS
ekckmr7qf8v5qj4v6ojmro2a3 *    manager1      Ready     Active          Leader
sfngbbh8ytw8smwvwldn2yq0q      testworker    Ready     Active
j97cjg16g4gwgpxz48dvg6h5o      worker1       Ready     Active
sbmurdxvyk7t3jqzncr9xrl5s      worker2       Ready     Active
docker@manager1:~$ 
```

Managing Services and Applications in a Swarm

Now that our cluster is ready, it's time to schedule some services on our cluster. As mentioned earlier, the role of the manager node is to accept Docker commands and apply them against the cluster. Therefore, we will create the services on the manager node.

 At this point, there really isn't much one can do on worker nodes as they are fully under the control of the manager.

Creating a Service

This command is used to create a service:

```
docker service create --replicas <count> -p <host_port>:<container_
port> --name <service_name> <image_name>
```

We run this on the manager as earlier alluded to. We are going to be using the WordPress example we built in the previous lesson. Since we already have this image locally, there will be no hassle pulling it from the hub.

Our replica count is going to be three because we currently have three worker nodes; confirm your node number by running `docker node ls`.

> We do not create a replica count; this introduces the following topics.The `-p` `<host_port>:<container_port>` maps the container to be built on our computer's defined port, against the container port. We do not need to have an equal number of replicas as our node number. Other nodes can handle different application layers, for example, the database:
>
> ```
> docker@manager1:~$ docker service create --replicas 3 -p 80:80 --name web wordpress
> fvc47jcitdgmv4t7ak60mqssa
> Since --detach=false was not specified, tasks will be created in the background.
> In a future release, --detach=false will become the default.
> docker@manager1:~$
> ```
>
> We created a web, based on the WordPress image, and mapped the host port `80` to the container port `80`.

Listing Services

This command is used to view the currently running services:

```
docker service ls
```

This command is used to view the currently running services and more information, such as the replicas, image, ports, and so on.

From the following output, we can see the service we just started and the associated information:

```
docker@manager1:~$ docker service ls
ID              NAME      MODE         REPLICAS    IMAGE              PORTS
fvc47jcitdgm    web       replicated   3/3         wordpress:latest   *:80->80/tcp
docker@manager1:~$
```

Service Status

This command is used to know whether our services are operational:

```
docker service ps <service_name>
```

Viewing the service listing will not provide us with all the information we need, such as what nodes our service is deployed on. However, we get to know whether our services are operational and the errors encountered, if any. When we run this on our manager, we get the following output:

 Viewing the status is very important. In a situation where we are running upgrades or updates on our nodes, running `docker ps` would inform us on the status of our nodes. In an ideal Docker Swarm setup, when a node goes down, the manager would reallocate traffic to the available nodes, thus it would be a little hard noticing downtime, unless monitoring is available. Before working with the nodes, always run this to check on the status of the nodes.

How Do We Know Our Site is Running?

We can verify WordPress is running by opening any of the workers' IP addresses on our browser:

```
→  Lesson-3 docker-machine ip worker1
192.168.99.102
→  Lesson-3
```

Here is a screenshot of how WordPress would appear on our browser:

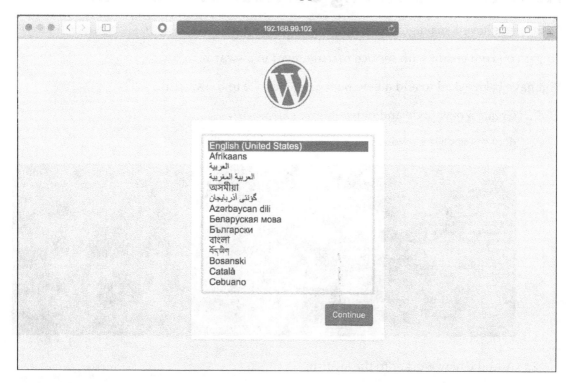

Opening any of the IP addresses running the WordPress web service, including the manager node, will open the same address.

Activity 2 — Running Services on a Swarm

Ensure you have a manager node running.

To get you conversant with service management in a swarm.

You have been asked to add a new `postgres` service to the swarm.

1. Create a new node and name it `dbworker`:

   ```
   docker-machine create --driver virtualbox dbworker
   ```

   ```
   → Lesson-3 docker-machine create --driver=virtualbox dbworker
   Running pre-create checks...
   Creating machine...
   (dbworker) Copying /Users/josephmuli/.docker/machine/cache/boot2docker.iso to /Users/josephmuli/.docker/machine/machines/dbworker/boot2docker.iso.
   (dbworker) Creating VirtualBox VM...
   (dbworker) Creating SSH key...
   (dbworker) Starting the VM...
   (dbworker) Check network to re-create if needed...
   (dbworker) Waiting for an IP...
   Waiting for machine to be running, this may take a few minutes...
   Detecting operating system of created instance...
   Waiting for SSH to be available...
   Detecting the provisioner...
   Provisioning with boot2docker...
   Copying certs to the local machine directory...
   Copying certs to the remote machine...
   Setting Docker configuration on the remote daemon...
   Checking connection to Docker...
   Docker is up and running!
   To see how to connect your Docker Client to the Docker Engine running on this virtual machine, run: docker-machine env dbworker
   ```

2. Add the new worker to the swarm:

   ```
   → Lesson-3 docker-machine ssh dbworker
                           ##         .
                     ## ## ##        ==
                  ## ## ## ## ##    ===
              /"""""""""""""""""\___/ ===
         ~~~ {~~ ~~~~ ~~~ ~~~~ ~~~ ~ /  ===- ~~~
              _____ o           __/
                \    \         __/
                 _____/


   ( ) (   ) (  )( )( )( )
   ( )( )( )( )(  )( )( )
   ( )( )( )(  )( )( )  (  )
   (  )( )( )( )( )  ( )

   Boot2Docker version 17.09.1-ce, build HEAD : e7de9ae - Fri Dec  8 19:41:36 UTC 2017
   Docker version 17.09.1-ce, build 19e2cf6
   docker@dbworker:~$ docker swarm join --token SWMTKN-1-1xk4mxwd7afjohspramr3qkbmp93es9pxl52vjitvbyoy4nmy4-71gjzypznjdkmkb631nov4yli 192.168.99.100:2377
   This node joined a swarm as a worker.
   docker@dbworker:~$
   ```

3. Create a new database service and name it `db`, using the postgres image as the base:

```
docker service create --replicas 1 --name db postgres
```

Here is a screenshot of the output:

4. Verify `postgres` is running through the following steps:

   1. Map the `postgres` container running in `dbworker node` to your computer:

   ```
   docker run --name db -e POSTGRES_PASSWORD=postgres -d -p
   5432:5432 postgres
   ```

   2. Run `docker ps` to list running containers; this should have our `postgres` container and the status should be UP:

   3. Exit and stop the container through the following:

Scaling Services Up and Down

As the number of requests coming into your application increases or decreases, there will be a need to scale the infrastructure. We have recently worked with node replicas running the same WordPress installation we made.

That is a very basic example of a production-level setup. Ideally, we would need a few more manager nodes and replicas, but since we are running a demo, this will be sufficient.

Scaling involves both the increase and decrease of resources depending on an application's traffic.

Scaling Our Database Service

We will scale our database service as an example of how to scale services. In a real-world scenario, cloud services such as Google Cloud Platform and Amazon Web Services may have automatic scaling services defined, where a number of replicas are created and traffic is distributed across the replicas through a service known as **load balancing**. We will dig deeper into that in the next activity. First, we understand how scaling works from the basics. The command for scaling the database is in the following format:

```
docker service scale <service_name>=<count>
```

To scale the service, pass in the service name we provided when creating the service and the number of replicas you want to increase it to.

The --detach=false allows us to view the replication progress. The command is docker service scale <service_name>=<count>:

From the output above, we can see that our db service has been replicated. We now have two database services running on the dbworker node.

How Does Swarm Know Where to Schedule a Service?

We covered scheduling modes earlier; they include the following:

- Random
- Spread
- Binpack

The default scheduling strategy for Docker Swarm is `spread`, which assigns a new service to the node with the least resources.

> If you don't have extra unassigned nodes on the swarm, the service you want to scale will be replicated on the currently running nodes.
>
> The swarm manager will use the spread strategy and allocate according to resources.

We can then verify that the action was indeed successful using the `docker service ls` command and we can see that the number of replicas is two:

```
docker@manager1:~$ docker service ls
ID              NAME      MODE          REPLICAS    IMAGE              PORTS
ek36eutnl1zz    db        replicated    2/2         postgres:latest
fvc47jcitdgm    web       replicated    3/3         wordpress:latest   *:80->80/tcp
```

Scaling down is pretty similar to scaling up, only we pass a lower replica count than we had before. From the following output, we scale down to one replica and verify that the replica count is one:

```
docker@manager1:~$ docker service scale --detach=false db=1
db scaled to 1
overall progress: 1 out of 1 tasks
1/1: running   [==================================================>]
verify: Service converged
docker@manager1:~$ docker service ls
ID              NAME      MODE          REPLICAS    IMAGE              PORTS
ek36eutnl1zz    db        replicated    1/1         postgres:latest
fvc47jcitdgm    web       replicated    3/3         wordpress:latest   *:80->80/tcp
```

How Does Swarm Load Balance Requests between Replicas?

A load balancer helps in handling and managing requests in an application. In cases where an application handles a lot of requests, which could be 1,000 in less than 5 minutes, we would need to have multiple replicas and a load balancer on our application, specifically the logical (backend) section. The load balancer helps distribute requests and prevent overloading of an instance, eventually leading to downtime.

When deploying to production on a cloud platform such as **Google Cloud Platform** or **Amazon Web Services**, you can make use of an external load balancer to route requests to your swarm hosts.

Docker Swarm includes a built-in routing service that enables each node in the swarm to accept incoming connections to a published port, even if there is no service running on the node. postgres service uses port 5432 by default.

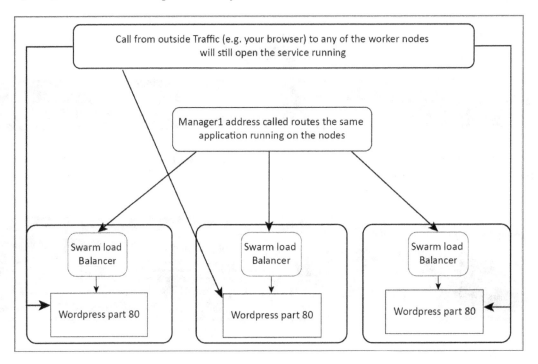

Activity 3 — Scaling Services on a Swarm

Ensure you have a swarm with at least one manager, two services, and three worker nodes.

To get you conversant with scaling services and replicating nodes.

You have been asked to scale the web service to four replicas and the database service to two replicas.

1. Create three new worker nodes, two for the web service and one for the database service.

2. Connect to the manager node and scale the web and database services.

3. Confirm the service replica count using docker service ls; the final result should be as follows:

    °   The WordPress web service should have two replica counts
    °   The Postgres database service should have four replica counts

Summary

In this lesson, we have done the following:

- Talked about orchestration and mentioned a few example tools
- Discussed clustering and why it's important, especially in production-level setups
- Learned about virtual hosts by running Docker Machines on VirtualBox
- Walked through Docker Swarm and how to create and manage a cluster of nodes
- Introduced example services including Wordpress running on our swarm
- Gained a high-level understanding of working with the `docker-machine cli`
- Talked about load balancing and how Docker Swarm manages this

Congratulations for getting to the finish line! Here's a recap of the knowledge we have gained through the lessons.

In this book, we have covered the following:

- Talked about DevOps and how Docker contributes to the workflow
- Understood how to template applications on Dockerfiles
- Built images and containers and pushed them to Docker Hub
- Managed containers through `docker-compose`
- Learned how we can orchestrate our applications through Docker Swarm

Index

www.ingramcontent.com/pod-product-compliance
Lightning Source LLC
Chambersburg PA
CBHW080541060326
40690CB00022B/5198